β18

# Rivers
# Alde, Ore and Blyth

## Vol. 3 English Estuaries Series

ROBERT SIMPER

Published in 1994 by Creekside Publishing

ISBN 0 9519927 3 2
© Robert Simper
Printed by The Lavenham Press Ltd
Lavenham, Suffolk

By the same author

*Over Snape Bridge* (1967)
*Woodbridge & Beyond* (1972)
*East Coast Sail* (1972)
*Scottish Sail* (1974)
*North East Sail* (1975)
*British Sail* (1977)
*Victorian & Edwardian Yachting from Old Photographs* (1978)
*Gaff Sail* (1979)
*Traditions of East Anglia* (1980)
*Suffolk Show* (1981)
*Britain's Maritime Heritage* (1982)
*Sail on the Orwell* (1982)
*Beach Boats of Britain* (1984)
*Sail. The Surviving Tradition* (1984)
*East Anglian Coast and Waterways* (1985)
*The Suffolk Sandlings* (1986)
*The Deben River* (1992)
*The River Orwell and the River Stour* (1993)

# CONTENTS

Cover: Edwin Gifford's *Ottor*, a half-size replica of a
tenth century Anglo-Saxon trading ship, at Snape.
Photograph by Pearl Simper.

# Acknowledgements

Although I had been to Orford several times, it was not until 1960 that I sailed up as far as Aldeburgh. As we approached Slaughden I was surprised to see a dinghy heading straight towards us. It was being rowed by a man in a peaked cap, brown smock and with gold earring and he seemed determined to get right under *Sea Fever's* bow. At the last moment I pushed the tiller away and narrowly missed the man in the boat. He was furious and roared at us.

'Little boats go to Loo'ward !'.

While I tried to work out what on earth he was shouting about, he passed us a card which welcomed us to Aldeburgh Yacht Club and offered us their hospitality. I felt a bit churlish at having given their boatman, 'Jumbo' Ward, such a close shave. Fortunately on the many occasions I met Jumbo after this he did not recognize me. From Jumbo I heard many stories, not just from his own memory, but tales he had heard as a boy from his grandfather 'Ducker' Ward who had gone to sea, aged nine, in 1854 on one of Newson Garrett's ships.

More memories of the halcyon days of Edwardian England just before World War I came from Henry Lucock. He grew up at Shingle Street in the days when the hamlet supported six pilots. He remembers going with his father William when he piloted barges up to Snape and the stops at the 'Three Mariners' at Slaughden on the way back. More and very different memories of that era came from Humphrey Rope whose family had been corn and coal merchants on Orford Quay.

Reg Snowden, Ralph Brinkley, Christine Bayly, Martin Eve, Geoffrey Ingram Smith, Richard Roberts and Elisabeth Russell all helped to bring the Orford story up to date. There is a marked rarity of early photographs of the River Ore, but further north the position changed because the Victorian visitors created a demand for photographs to take home to remind them of their wonderful holidays on the Suffolk coast. It is very noticeable that there are more paintings available, particularly from nineteenth century Walberswick and in the more modern period around Aldeburgh than on other parts of the Suffolk coast. The fact that a major arts festival takes places in Aldeburgh means that artistic appreciation is far higher than in the average small town.

At Aldeburgh Billy Burrell talked about the fishing and Clair Foss was a great help with photographs she has filed in the Moot Hall. Peter Wilson had a great store of knowledge about yachting. The past around the head of the River Alde has been thoroughly researched by Mary Harrison of Snape who found the Roman salt pans and helped set up the Snape Historical Trust which undertook the dig on the Anglo-Saxon burial site. The interpretation of the Snape dig comes from its director, William Filmer-Sankey. Sam Newton and John Newman helped to keep me on course with the Anglo-Saxons.

At Southwold, Eric Paisley and the harbour master Ken Howells were most helpful and John Winter and John 'Wiggie' Goldsmith provided a wealth of information. At Walberswick Ruth Goodwin helped, and on the River Blyth, Cliff Waller, and Dick Collett of Blythburgh remembered the days when there were wherries in the Blyth. Graham Newman passed on stories from families in the Halesworth Quay area and John E.B. Hill also helped. I also found Wilfrid J. Wren's *Ports of the Eastern Counties* useful.

I am particularly grateful to David Green of Woodbridge who has gone to a great deal of trouble to provide atmospheric drawings of the estuaries. Thanks to Ron van den Bos for the Snape Maltings map which he drew years ago after seeing my *Over Snape Bridge*. Geoff Cordy provided his usual reliable service with photographs. My daughter Caroline Southernwood helped with illustrations and my wife Pearl did more than anyone else to help draw this project to its conclusion.

R.S.
Ramsholt

**Source of illustrations**

David Green 1,2, 3, 4. Humphrey Rope 5, 37, 38, 39, 40. Cliff Hoppitt 6, 21, 71a, 78, 85, 96. Jane Parsey 7, 8. Henry Lucock 9. F.Hussey 10. National Rivers Authority 11, 12, 23, 67, 74, 75, 87. Anne Bantoft 15, 16. D.Royston Booth 18, 19. East Anglian Daily Times 20, 53, 53a, 113, 135. Jonathan Simper 21a, 134a. John Hewitt 25, 26. Suffolk Photo Survey 28, 77. Pearl Simper 30. Richard Roberts 31, 43. Christine Bayly 32, 33, 41, 79. RSPB/C.H.Gomersall 35. Elizabeth Russell 42, 45, 46, 47. Reg Snowden 44. Nicolas Minifie 56, 97. Aldeburgh Moot Hall 58, 60, 61, 62, 63, 66, 76. Mary Harrison 48, 65. Peter Wilson 70, 71, 72. Ron van den Bos 86. John Goldsmith 100, 101, 102, 105, 107, 108, 109, 110, 112, 112a, 114, 115, 116, 117, 118, 119, 120, 121, 123, 125, 126, 134. Eric Paisley 124, 125. John Cragie 103, 104. N.Hutton 106. John Winter 127. Geoff Cordy 85a, 129, 131, 137. Graham Newman 138. The rest were taken by the author or are from his collection.

# Chapter One

# THE SHIFTING COAST

It was one of those hot summer afternoons and we went down to Shingle Street for a swim. Following the war time road out in front of the houses, we passed the ponds and arrived at the beach. As the tide receded the remains of the wooden bow of a sailing ship was revealed in the breaking water. It was, I learnt decades later, the wreck of the schooner *Rudolph*. She had been the largest vessel trading into the Alde-Ore and had been owned by Captain Ned Norton of Slaughden. William Lucock, one of the Shingle Street pilots, had been helping to bring her in, but somehow the *Rudolph*, with 230 tons of coal aboard, managed to sit on her anchor while waiting for the tide. She never floated again and was broken up where she lay.

The *Rudolph* was wrecked in about 1903 and her hull was eventually buried by shingle. When I saw her wreck, possibly half a century after her final voyage, the entrance of the river had moved back north about half a mile. The mouth of the Alde-Ore estuary on the Suffolk coast at Shingle Street is constantly moving. When Orford Castle was built in 1156 it was just below Orford. In nearly seven hundred years the river mouth had moved south five miles so that it was flowing out on the Bawdsey side of Shingle Street. In 1896 a storm closed this mouth with shingle and the river burst out again opposite the old 'Life Boat Inn' roughly in the middle of the hamlet.

Further movement of the mouth resulted in the shingle being eroded away from in front of the houses. In 1965 there was a massive operation with lorries and diggers to pile shingle up in front of the Coast Guard Cottages to stop the encroachment. The sea then ate its way inland a little further to the south to reach a point where in a big gale it was throwing driftwood right up to the garden fences and the sea filtered under the houses to flood the road behind it. After a while the shingle started piling up again.

It is not just at Shingle Street that the coast line alters, the whole Suffolk coast constantly changes. It happens very slowly, but every generation sees a little bit more land slide into the sea. If a Roman sailor or a raiding Viking could return to the Suffolk coast they would not recognise it. In many places the coastline has receded a mile or more. Erosion has completely altered the estuaries that flow out into the North Sea. The Dunwich-Blyth river was a long estuary flowing out into a huge natural harbour of which only the short Blyth remains. On the other hand the Alde has been added to by almost all the length of the Ore. At Orford and Aldeburgh the same river had a different name because the people had very little contact with each other.

The loss of land through erosion has been far greater than most people realise. When standing on the sea defences at Slaughden it seems hard to believe that the River Alde did not have a mouth here. In fact there used to be about half a mile of land in front of this point. The Alde always turned south. The remains of these old southern channels which are now out under the sea, came back into the present Orford Ness to join the estuary at Pig's Pail and the larger Stony Ditch. When the channel carved its way inland Orford Ness did not become an island. 'The Island', which is in fact a peninsular only got this name from 'newcomers' who moved into Orford in the 1920s.

Nothing on this coast ever stays the same. The Alde-Ore estuary channel moved at will over a vast plain of saltings until medieval walling confined it to its present channel. As Orford Ness extended and the River Ore grew longer, mud banks formed in mid channel. In about 1450 these banks were walled to create Havergate and Dovey Islands. Much later the silt built up and linked both islands. The Orfordness shingle peninsular continued to extend south and by 1590 the shingle had passed the Butley River mouth, making that river a tributary of the Ore. It did the same to Hollesley Haven which then silted up and became Barthorp's Creek.

Because of the great length of the Alde-Ore river there was always a large volume of water forcing its way out through the mouth. Smaller estuaries were not so lucky. Lost rivers such as Thorpe Haven, Minsmere Haven, Frostenden River and even the remains of the Dunwich River all had their mouths closed. There was not enough weight of water to burst through the shingle which was dragged across their mouths by severe gales.

While the rivers choked up, other places slipped into the sea. The little hamlet of Minsmere has gone. The sandy cliffs it stood on have long since collapsed into the sea. Minsmere Haven has turned into marshes which are now an RSPB reserve. Easton Bavents has also gone, not just the village but the long sandy headland it

1. The *Credo* on a Southwold landing stage, 1993. By David Green.

once stood on. Here the sea still carves its way inland and there is nothing left to show that this was once the most easterly point in Britain. At Dunwich the story is even more dramatic, the whole town was eaten up by the sea.

The proud town of Dunwich which in the early medieval period was the fourth largest city in Britain owed its success to the fact that it sat beside the finest natural harbour on the east coast. From Dunwich, ships sailed all over northern Europe and to the lucrative Icelandic cod fishery bringing wealth and power to the town's merchants and employment to its people. When the cliffs at Dunwich started to slide into the sea the townspeople fought back. Every autumn, bushwood faggots were placed at the cliff foot and they managed to hold back the sea for several generations. Then in 1328 a great storm threw shingle across the harbour mouth. The men of Dunwich dug a new entrance by hand, but the harbour was never as good as the original one. Ships had difficulty getting to Dunwich and trade drifted away. No revenue was then available to continue sea defence projects. By the end of the eighteenth century all that remained of the medieval town was the cliff top ruins and a few

bits of masonry scattered about on the sea bed. Dunwich was such a good harbour that, had it survived into modern times, funds would have been made available to save it.

After Dunwich harbour was closed, Walberswick, Blythburgh and Southwold fought over the trade. The men of Southwold won this struggle when they cut a gully to give the River Blyth another mouth which was within their parish boundaries. Much later, in the eighteenth century, piers were built at the mouth of the Blyth to try and make Southwold a good haven for shipping. These piers greatly slowed down the coastal erosion, although they did not stop it completely. The Southwold fishermen's beach village, where some sixteen families lived in the mid-Victorian era, was largely swept away by the beginning of the twentieth century. The rest of Southwold, thanks to its piers and sea defences has survived.

Erosion has done more than just eat away a town and a few villages on the Suffolk coast. It has had a profound economic and social effect. The great medieval churches of Orford, Aldeburgh, Walberswick, Southwold and Blythburgh were expressions of local wealth derived from trade

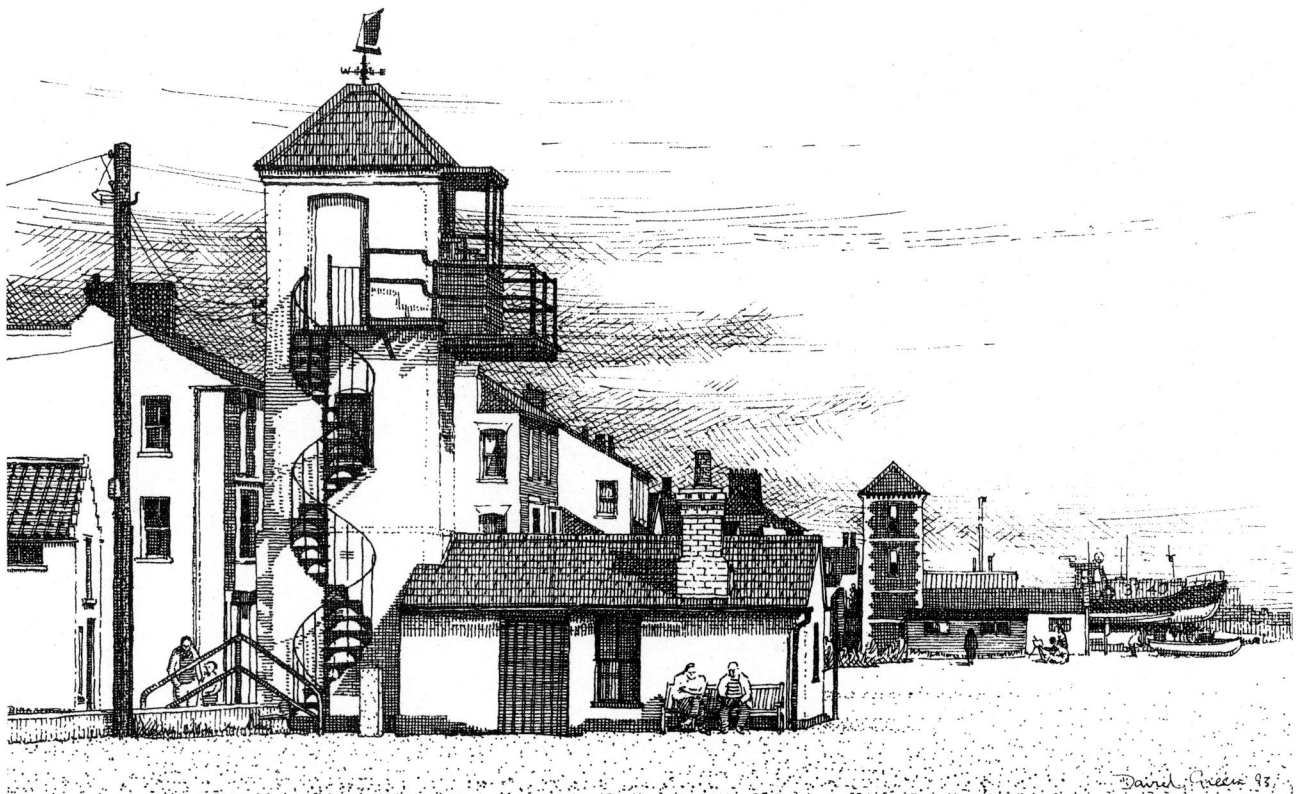

2. The South Company or 'Up towners' lookout at Aldeburgh by David Green, 1993. In the distance is the North Company or 'Down towners' look out. These were the headquarters of two nineteenth century beach companies or fishermen's cooperatives. At Aldeburgh these companies were mainly involved in putting Thames Estuary pilots on ships until 1899. There was another lookout on the high ground at Aldeburgh but these two on the beach are the last East Anglian beach company lookouts.

3. Orford Quay. By David Green, 1993.

and fishing. Later generations knew that Dunwich had been washed away and were worried that their town would be next. People lost faith and moved.

The little ports on the Alde-Ore and Blyth are, to my mind, some of the most attractive in England, but they are failed commercial centres. Because trade drifted away the sleepy streets of these lovely places saw great poverty. To add insult to injury, the Reform Bill of 1832 robbed the Suffolk coastal ports of their ancient privileges. Orford, Aldeburgh and Dunwich were classed as 'Rotten Boroughs' and lost their Members of Parliament and eventually their borough status. It was not the town's people who were rotten in any way but the ancient system of borough privileges which were abused by a few powerful individuals.

In modern times some authors have suggested that the decline of Southwold was linked to the greed of a few powerful local land-lowners in the Blyth valley. They walled off the tidal Blyth saltings to rent them out for cattle grazing. This reduced the amount of water that flowed in and out. But it was not as simple as that, Southwold Harbour always had problems with silting before the walling, and after many of the walls had collapsed. The mouth of the Harbour has had to be cleared of shingle more times than the town cares to remember, but Southwold people have doggedly fought on over the centuries to keep the port open.

In the late eighteenth century there was a sudden burst of prosperity at Southwold after the Harbour piers were built. Lowestoft harbour was not built until the nineteenth century so the British Free Fishery went to Southwold. This had been a state venture to try and challenge the Dutch dominance of the North Sea herring fishery. The British Free Fishery failed after a few years, amongst cries that the management had been corrupt. The opening of the navigation up to Halesworth in 1761 certainly helped local trade, but because shingle kept closing Southwold Harbour, large scale industry would not come near the port. Inshore fishing has thrived from this Harbour bringing employment to the Southwold area and adding a sense of purpose and atmosphere to the waterside.

The Suffolk coast's long period of economic isolation ended when the railways arrived. Branch lines reached Aldeburgh in 1860 and Southwold in 1879 and even Snape had a little line going down to the Maltings. The railways, even the slow narrow gauge Southwold Railway, made it possible for fishermen to send their catch to the London markets. Before this only a little fresh fish was sold locally, usually by women, and the rest had to be smoked. In 1819 Aldeburgh had seventeen 'drying houses' where smoking produced the red sprats and other smoked fish, primarily for export to Holland.

The railways brought in summer visitors which turned Aldeburgh and Southwold into

4. Shingle Street. By David Green, 1994.

genteel seaside resorts. Only Orford remained a village, because the railway did not reach it, although by the end of the nineteenth century tourists were arriving here by horse drawn coaches. The coastal area had retained its own clear identity quite separate from the rest of England. People still spoke their own version of the English language. In pure Suffolk, Southwold was 'Suff'old', Walberswick 'Wozer'wick', Slaughden 'Slaughton', Gedgrave 'Ged'gr'ove', Hollesley 'Ho'esly' and so on.

The first summer visitors were delighted by the Sandlings coast. The rivers and villages between Shingle Street and Southwold were largely untouched by the industrial revolution. Walberswick, a rustic and impoverished fishing village, attracted so many artists that it almost had its own school of painters. Many of the wealthy Victorian visitors loved the slow moving life on the Suffolk coast and began to settle here. A new age was starting to dawn in which this coastal area became within reach of the great wealth of south east England.

The Blyth areas long period of commercial isolation might have ended in 1906 when Fasey & Son bought Southwold Harbour. Helped by Government grants, they tried to develop it as a fish landing station to rival Lowestoft and Yarmouth. Faseys built a new quay and a fish market and for a few years some of the North Sea herring fleet landed their fish here. However there was considerable local opposition to the fish market. Some influential people did not like a London firm owning the harbour and the building of the branch line to it was delayed. The fish market scheme collapsed all to soon. The story of lost opportunities happened over and over again at Southwold, although in the end it created a lovely little residential town.

In 1936 Southwold Corporation tried again to improve it's Harbour. They bought the Harbour back and gave a Dutch firm the contract to rebuild it. Again there were strong local protests, particularly from Walberswick where some of the quay and warehouses were levelled. Unfortunately this scheme did not solve the problem because gales still left shingle across the harbour mouth. It was not until 1963 that the Southwold Borough Council obtained enough grants to make another attempt at the harbour mouth.

In the local government reorganization of 1974 the ownership of Southwold Harbour passed to Waveney District Council. The Waveney DC came up with a plan to solve Southwold's age old problems. They decided to let a Developer build a marina and holiday village on the Town Marshes. At a public meeting in 1986 the developer tried to tell a very hostile gathering of town's people his plans for their future. His words were drowned by a chant of GO NOW, and go he did. Just in case he returned there were cards left in many Southwold windows with the uncompromising message 'We Live Southwold. Stop Them.'

The pressure from residents, whose income did not always come from the local economy directly, affected the coastal villages and towns. This situation was both good and bad. The demand for tranquillity kept up house prices but drove manual workers and their places of employment out of some waterside areas. The demand for tourism facilities and yacht moorings at Orford, Aldeburgh and Southwold far exceeded the level that residents allowed. The estuaries of the Alde-Ore and Blyth have a very fragile beauty but inspite of all the changes and pressures these two tideways have retained their wild isolation which makes them unique.

# Chapter Two

# SHINGLE STREET AND THE BUTLEY RIVER

Oreford Haven.
1893

5.'Oreford Haven' in 1893 when the entrance was still to the south. The barges are in front of the Shingle Street Coast Guard station.

6. Shingle Street in 1985. The V shaped building in the foreground is the Battery built in the nineteenth century to guard the entrance of the River Ore.

Shingle Street, Hollesley - Suffolk.

7. Shingle Street seen from the Martello Tower in about 1928. The New Ponds (old river mouth) were still in front of the houses and the *Lifeboat Inn* is the two storey building in the centre. The first houses were built at Shingle Street, often of drift wood, in about 1810. The hamlet was then linked by a track along the beach to Bawdsey. Drinking water was caught from the rooves and stored in under ground tanks. Later there was a track across the marshes linking Shingle Street with Hollesley and water was sometimes brought in by horse and tumbril.

The men at Shingle Street were primarily fishermen, but they also picked up a living piloting or loading barges at Boyton Dock, or with shingle from the North Weir. In the 1880s there was also a salvage company here run by Francis Langmaid of the *Lifeboat Inn* which operated the yawl *Jane*.

Because of the threat of an imminent German invasion at the beginning of World War II most of the people were moved out of Shingle Street and the fishing boats were sunk by military order. After the war Henry Beeton rebuilt some houses for the Government, but Shingle Street never recovered as a fishing community.

8. The Royal Navy coastal defence gun at Shingle Street about 1915. The Coast Guard Station cottages in the backgound were the homes of eight men and their families.

9. At Shingle Street the large house on the sea front is the *Lifeboat Inn*. Next to the *Lifeboat* is Lucock's cottage with a figurehead from a wreck in the garden and then Frank Norton's cottage. The *Lifeboat* was destroyed in a bouncing bomb experiment early in World War II. A Hurrican flew in from the sea and dropped the bomb on the beach. This bounced up and crashed into the *Lifeboat* and exploded. The inventor Barnes Wallis, who had been standing on the beach watching, went in and inspected the impact and came out throwing his hands up in the air with delight at the success of the bomb.

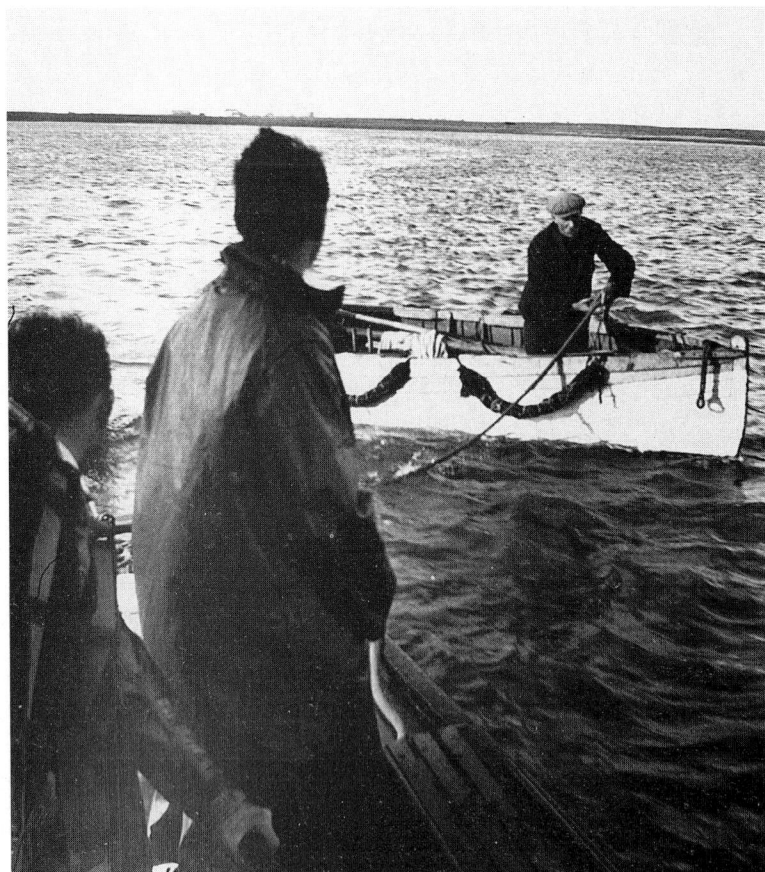

10. William Lucock, a pilot at Shingle Street, leaving Frank Hussey's yacht in 1930 after piloting her in. The last Shingle Street pilot was Eric Andrews. He went off to yachts in his boat *Gem* until the 1960s after which he flagged boats in from the beach.

11. Here in March 1949 a tidal surge is pushing water over the river wall at the entrance to Barthorpe Creek and flooding the Oxley Marshes.

12. The same tidal surge at Shingle Street in 1949.

13. The Mansion at Shingle Street in 1972. This was a holiday home originally called the German Ocean Mansion. The term German Ocean was dropped after World War I and the sea became known as the North Sea.

14. This photograph shows the shingle street in front of the houses at the hamlet of Shingle Street, 1990. Windy Ridge on the right is one of the cottages that survived World War II when the hamlet was used as a RAF practice bombing range.

15. Frogs Hall, farm on the edge of the Boyton Marshes, was completely levelled just after World War II. The drinking water for the people who lived at Frogs Hall came from a 'pulk', a Suffolk word meaning a small pond.

16. Sheep grazing on the saltings beside the Butley River in about 1930 with Boyton Dock in the background. The sheep were put on the saltings in the late summer to improve their fertility.

17 (above). Butley ferryman Bryan Rodgers with Graham Hussey's *Horace & Hannah* behind, beating up the Butley River, 1993. There was a ferry operating across the Butley River until about 1919. The ferry house was near Barrow Hill and on the other shore there was a bell to summons the ferry. In 1993 Sir Edward Greenwell, who owned the ferry right and the bed of the Butley River, supplied the material, and Bryan Rodgers repaired the hards and reopened the ferry. The old hard on the Gedgrave shore is buried under two feet of silt. In the first season the new Butley Ferry averaged two passengers a week.

The 19ft *Horace & Hannah* YH 321 was a Great Yarmouth shrimper built in 1907, but by the time Graham bought her she was a wreck. Between 1983–88 Graham and his son Dan rebuilt the *Horace & Hannah* at Neutral Farm, Butley and totally restored the shrimper to her original working appearance. The narrow tidal Butley River and Ore are very similar to the conditions in Yarmouth Harbour where the shrimpers sailed from.

18 (left). Richard Pinney with oyster baskets beside the Butley River in about 1965. Richard Pinney had been in publishing and fund raising in London and came up to Suffolk in 1947. After settling beside the Butley River in a cottage at Gedgrave he looked round for some method of earning a living there. First he cut and sold reeds, a business which grew into Debenham Rush Weavers and by 1958 he was producing oysters commercially in the Butley River.

19 (right). Loading oysters at Gedgrave Cliff on to Richard Pinney's *Mouche* in about 1965. Oysters, both native and Portuguese were fattened in the Butley River. During the very severe winter of 1962–63 ice blocks killed most of the oysters here but the fishery survived. These oysters were mostly sold through the Butley-Orford Oysterage which the Pinneys started on the Market Hill, Orford. There were not many good restaurants in rural Suffolk then and the Oysterage soon became, not just a local favourite, but attracted national attention in newspapers and magazines.

20 (below). Richard Pinney in his smoke house at the Ferry Cottage, Gedgrave about 1967. Smoking fish in order to preserve them had been practiced on the Suffolk coast since at least the medieval period. Richard enriched this tradition and promoted the sale of smoked fish as a delicacy.

21a. Eel fisherman Alan between dredging William Pinney's oysters off Gedgrave Cliff, Butley River, 1994.

21. The Butley River winding down to the River Ore in 1985. In the foreground is the causeway leading to Burrow Hill. Before the river walls existed Burrow Hill was an island with The Tang (river) running down the far side. The causeway might have been built across the marshes when there was an Iron Age settlement on the hill. In the 1930s William Turner of Home Farm, Capel St Andrew farmed the Burrow Hill land. His cattle always fattened well here, possibly because they moved round and could always graze in a sheltered spot.

22 (above). Excavations on Burrow Hill in 1986. The Butley Abbey monks called this hill 'Island of the Burgh' (fort), however a sand pit was dug in the middle of the settlement site. Sir Peter Greenwell closed this sand pit so that Valerie Fenwick could excavate the site. It was discovered that there had been a large Anglo-Saxon settlement here between 680–840. This had been largely a self sufficient community that even obtained iron from Gedgrave Cliff. The Anglo-Saxons probably abandoned Burrow Hill when the Great Viking army moved through East Anglia.

23 (right). The Chillesford Lodge marsh mill in 1947. This windmill pump was used instead of a sluice to move fresh water from the Fleet into the Butley River. While Amos Clarke was repairing the mill in 1920 the marsh flooded and he was marooned in the mill. Amos Clarke came out of retirement to repair this mill for Mr Alastair Watson in 1952. However during a gale in 1959 the sails and cap were blown away.

15

24. About 1927 Alastair Watson had the old harness room for the Sudbourne Hall Estate's Suffolk horses placed beside the Butley River as a bathing hut. Around the same time Ipswich barge skipper Harold Smy brought a sailing barge loaded with shingle up here to build the Chillesford Lodge stables, however this proved so difficult that Smy took further shipments to Orford Quay. In the 1930s George Brinkley brought shingle up here by launch for the Lodge drive.

25. A sailing barge at the head of the Butley River discharging rolled wheat for animal 'feed' for the Hewitt's in about 1908.

26. Butley miller E.T. Hewitt and family and friends aboard a barge just below Butley mill.

27. Reeds being cut at the head of the Butley River, 1990. The reeds are cut in the winter after a frost has killed the green growth.

# Chapter Three

# ORFORD AND IT'S BLEAK ISLANDS

28. The Orford Ness Low Light was washed away in 1887 by a big storm that also broke through Orford Beach and flooded the marshes around the Butley River. The first two light houses were built on Orford Ness after a bad storm in 1661 when thirty-two ships were lost with most of their crews on Orford Ness. The two lights were built so that ships coming south could line them up and get safely through the sandbanks off Aldeburgh. After the nineth Low Light house was washed away Trinity House decided to replace it with a new lighthouse at Southwold.

29. The High Lighthouse on Orford Ness was built in 1792. Here the Customs Landrover stuck briefly while on a drugs patrol. At one stage the Customs Officer lived in Aldeburgh and used to walk the five miles down to the light house on the Ness. Walkers on the shingle put their heels down first.

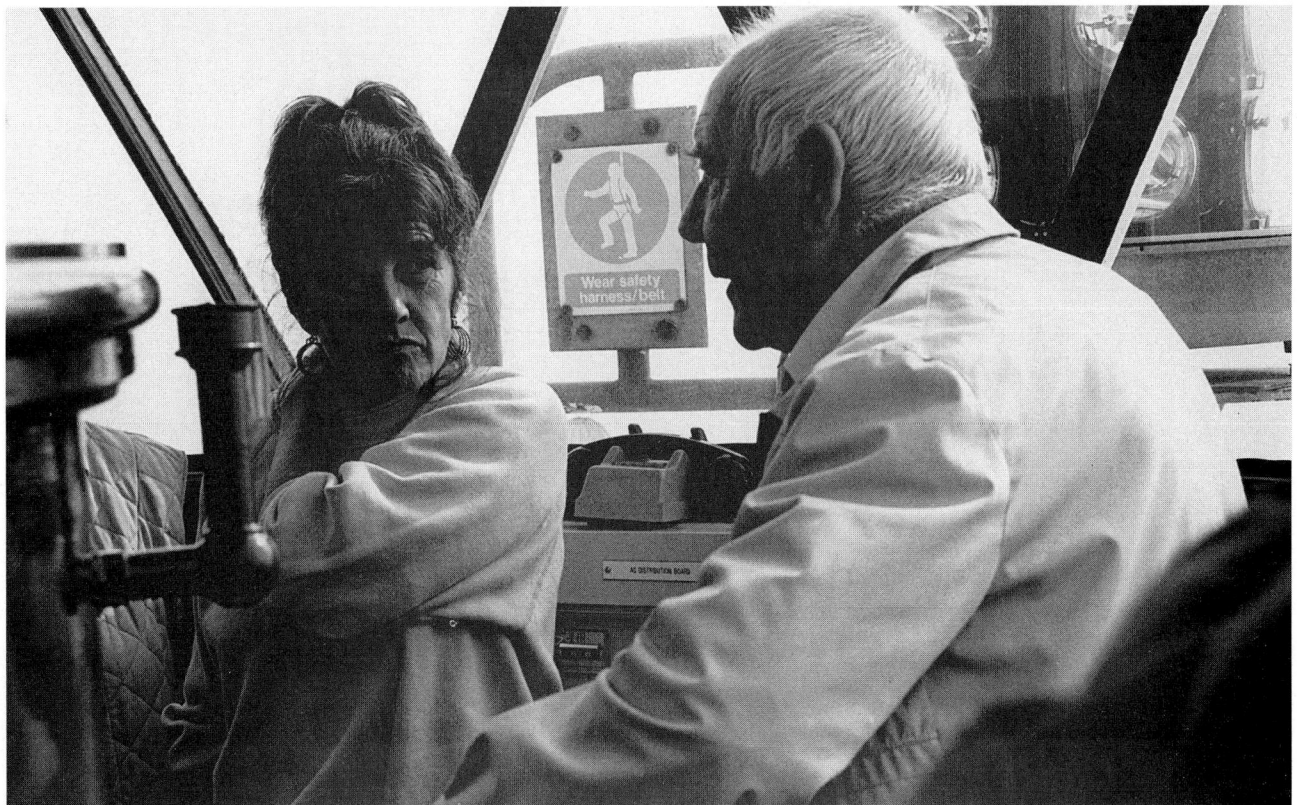

30. Charlie Underwood right, in the light chamber of Orford Ness light house explaining how the light operated, 1992. Charlie Underwood became the attendant for Orford Ness lighthouse when it became automatic in 1965. He lives in Orford and goes across to maintain the lighthouse which is actually controlled from Harwich.

31. R.A. Roberts and some of his family on the railway to Orford Ness, 1929. Roberts had bought the Smithy Cottage at Orford in 1923 when Sudbourne Hall Estate was breaking up. Built in 1928 the railway ran from the Air Force Quay across to the beach and was used to service the new experimental station. Orford Ness became very 'hush hush' and a very secret place until 1971.

32. The cottage on Havergate Island about 1922. From the right is Robert Brinkley and his son William. Both these men were marsh keepers who dug ditches and made up river walls in the winter and looked after the cattle in the summer. The cottage was divided for two families and there was a small barn on the saltings. Havergate belonged to the Fiskes of Bramford and on the left are some members of this family.

33. Robert Brinkley, seen here at the Havergate Cottage which was built about 1780. The Brinkleys moved from Orford on to Havergate in about 1880. The wife of the previous marsh keeper Elizabeth Smith, gave birth to four of their children, on Havergate.

In the Victorian period many country people lived hard and lonely lives. Brinkley's brother lived over on Orford Ness in a similar cottage, so that Havergate did not seem unusual. There was, however, little contact with the outside world except a weekly visit via the Horse Hard to Orford, for stores. If the postman had some letters for the Brinkleys a flag was hoisted near the Horse Hard and they rowed across the Gull to collect them. The whole family used to go beach-combing on Orford Ness after a gale and they had boats to go fishing in. Robert Brinkley must have liked Havergate because he stayed there until he died in 1924. William Brinkley stayed on his own for six months and then Mr Welham and his house keeper Alice Ellis lived there for about two more years. Noone has lived on Havergate permanently since then, although RSPB wardens often stay there.

34. From this Horse Hard, in the Upper Gull, cattle and horses had to swim across to graze on Havergate. By 1910 a small barge, which ended up as one of Ralph Brinkley's sheds at Orford Quay, was being used to take cattle across to Havergate. First this was hauled across by huge blocks and tackle and then until 1953 by Vic Brinkley's boat. Horses also had to swim across at Orford 'over the other side' to the Orford Ness marshes until a large lighter, rowed by two men on platforms, was introduced.

The 267 acre Havergate Island is two miles long and carried about 400 head of cattle for summer grazing. About 1937 Reg Snowden was one of a gang of men hired by a drover to take cattle from Havergate to Beccles. At low water they brought 250 cattle across to Horse Hard and then with the help of dogs walked the cattle to Yoxford and the next day they went on to Beccles.

35. An avocet on Havergate. During World War II the gunners on the Boyton Marshes sometimes missed their targets and blew gaps in Dovey wall and flooded the lower end of Havergate. The flooded marshes created shallow lagoons which provided just the right habitat for the lovely avocets. For the first time for over a century avocets stayed and nested on Havergate and at Minsmere. Because of this the Royal Society for the Protection of Birds purchased Havergate in 1947 and started their first wild life reserve.

36. John Partridge, RSPB warden for Havergate, landing from the *October Storm* on the island in 1993. Reg Partridge started as the first full time warden in 1949 and John followed after his father's death in 1974.

# Bought of EDWARD ROPE,
## Brewers' Agent, Spirit, Corn and Coal Merchant.

Agent for Truman, Hanbury & Co.'s Stout; Salt & Co.'s and Marston's Burton Ales.

LINSEED AND COTTON CAKES.    AGENT FOR THE "ALLIANCE" INSURANCE OFFICE.

*Sacks, Casks, Cases, Hampers and Bottles, if not returned within Six Months, to be paid for.*
AGENT FOR LAWES' CHEMICAL MANURES.
ACCOUNTS RENDERED QUARTERLY.    5 per cent. per annum charged on accounts of over 6 months' standing.

37. Edward Rope rented Orford Quay from the Sudbourne Hall Estate and ran a business as a malster, brewer, corn and coal merchant here. At one time he also ran a similar business at Slaughden Quay. Rope also had the Quay Street brewery, the 'Jolly Sailor' and 'King's Head' at Orford and the 'Oyster' at Butley. After Edward's death his family remained living at the Quay House. Edward's son Walter took over the business until in was sold in 1921.

38. The Rope's summer bungalow or 'cabin' built on a boat beside the Stony Ditch in about 1910.

39. Walter Rope about to ferry two of his sisters across the Stony Ditch. When Walter's family were alone at the cabin the children ran about naked, but when the spinster aunts arrived, this was strictly forbidden.

40. Charlie Stoker's smack *Winona* at Orford in about 1930. The Romans certainly enjoyed oysters when they lived around the Alde. In the medieval period there were oysters above Slaughden and as the river grew longer new beds of native oysters appeared in the Ore. By royal charter Orford owned all the river bed and fish within its parish boundaries. This was upheld at a hearing at Bury St Edmunds Assizes in 1791 following a raid by fifty two smacks from Brightlingsea. They came to dredge oysters freely from below Havergate right up to Orford. Soon after this the Marquis of Hertford, as Lord of the Manor, charged eighty smacks a guinea a year each to dredge in the 'considerable' Orford Oyster Fishery.

Orford lost its two Members of Parliament in 1832, but the Borough leased out the oyster fishery to a shareholder company who appears to have worked oysters in the Narrows and had oyster pits in the Stony Ditch. In 1883 the Borough was abolished and its property taken over by the Orford Town Trust from whom the Ropes leased the oyster fishery until 1920. About 1926 MacFisheries took on the lease, Charlie Stoker came round from West Mersea to look after the fishery and Tom Eve managed it. Portuguese schooners brought oysters to the Butley River for fattening and the 1885 storage pits at Gedgrave Cliff were used. The slump of 1930 resulted in MacFisheries abandoning the Orford fishery.

24

41. Some of the men who founded the Dabchick Sailing Club at Orford in 1924. Left to right– G. Brinkley, J. Lewis, F. Chambers, W. Green. G. Whayman, V. Brinkley, T. Brinkley.

42. Regatta Day at Orford in 1938 with Tomtits and other yachts racing down river and Tom Rigg's *Alan* at anchor. A Dutch coaster is discharging coal at the Quay. The Orford Regatta was started in 1877 and in the 1930s it was supported by the whole town. Only later did a gulf between the old and new town grow up.

43. Mrs Roberts and her sister Mrs Matthews with their children returning back to Orford after a trip to Iken Cliff, 1929.

44. Unloading coal for Charles Friend on Orford Quay in 1935. On the left is Reg Snowden with the horse, Fred Borrett is in the little lorry and the harbour master George Brinkley behind it. The Orford coal merchant Charles Friend had seven barge loads of coal delivered to the Quay during the summer until 1939. Sailing barges and small coasters are remembered, bringing freights of about 150 tons of coal from Hull. The gang needed to unload a barge at Orford was two men in the hold filling the 2 cwt baskets, one man on deck working the hand winch and another tipping the basket into the cart. Two men with horses and tumbrils and a lorry man took the coal to the sheds where another two men shovelled up the coal for storage. Coal was sold round the villages in the winter. It took three days to unload a barge and the men were paid thirty shillings for this, which was more than they earnt all week on the farms, but it was hard work.

45. George Brinkley and Betty Johnson, later Mrs Elisabeth Russell, after the 1937 Whitson Race at the Orford Dabchick Sailing Club. George Brinkley was born on Orford Ness and did not go to school.

46. Alex Comins and family friends on a picnic trip to the lower Ore with his Tomtit *Tania* in 1951.

47. After the East Coast Floods of 1953 the tide poured through a break in the river wall just below Orford Quay.

48. Looking from Orford towards the Butley River before the 1953 flood water had receded.

49. The Watch House on Orford Quay in 1973 when it was still a Coast Guard station. A telescope was used to watch the sea from the upstairs window. and rocket life saving apparatus was stored in the lower floor. During World War II an Observer Corp post was built on top of the building to spot enemy aircraft coming in over the coast.

50. The Orford Town Trust oyster packing shed in 1973 when there were still oyster dredges stored in the loft. In the foreground is the remains of the oyster storage shed which had a pit that filled with the tide. The Ropes used the shed for packing oysters,a score (twenty) in every bag, ready for sale. MacFisheries also packed and retailed oysters from this shed. A room was built on the back of the 'Jolly Sailor' for the Thursdays 'Stout and Orford Oyster' evenings.

51. The Orford Ness ferry *Portree* LCGF 4 at Orford in 1973. She was here until 1990 and was the largest of four ferries stationed here when the Ministry of Defence ran the ferry service to the secret Atomic Weapons Research Establishment over on The Island.

Most of the traffic to the Island was lorries, cars and foot passengers for the MOD and World Service, but in the summer, cattle were taken over to graze the marshes. The ferry was supposed to carry sixteen cattle but once twenty were put in to speed up the operation. All the cattle went and stood in the bows and the ferry arrived with her bows 2ft under water much to the alarm of her crew. Cattle grazing on the island was suspended in 1990.

52. Ferry heading for Orford Quay in 1992. Alongside the Quay is the 50ft passenger boat *Lady Florence* which was built at Poole in 1944 as an Admiralty supply vessel.

30

53. Geoffrey Ingram Smith at the wheel of the *Lady Florence*. This was during one of the river trips from Orford Quay that he started and ran between 1984–1992. Geoffrey bought the Watch House on Orford Quay and the MFV *Progress* after this.

53a. Lunch on the *Lady Florence*. Orford has a reputation for providing good inexpensive food.

54. Peter Weir's *Regardless* leaving Orford Quay for another trip round Havergate Island. He started running these trips with this new wooden boat in 1992.

55. Steve Richardson in 1994 with herring at his Orford smoke house. Steve started working for Richard Pinney in the Butley river oyster layings, then worked abroad before he returned to Orford to restart the smoke house in Baker's Lane. Steve's grandfather Frank Berrett had operated this before 1939.

In the 1970s William Pinney was sea fishing from the Butley River in a small fast boat. This progressed on so that by 1994 there were five fast boats based at Orford, some capable of twenty-four knots. These flat bottomed boats worked up to forty miles off shore with longlines or buoyed nets.

## Chapter Four

# SLAUGHDEN POUND TO COB ISLAND

56. The Aldeburgh cod smack *Lady Montefiore* leaving Aldeburgh about 1901. The fishery dated back to the medieval period when Walberswich, Dunwich, Aldeburgh, Orford and Ipswich had all sent ships to Icelandic waters. For four hundred years the vessels sailed to Iceland and into the North Sea grounds to longline for cod and ling. Because of the lack of other opportunities, Aldeburgh continued on with this deep water longlining fleet long after other ports had gone over to trawlers. Often the Aldeburgh tradesmen clubbed together and bought a smack just to give employment in the town and help the hard pressed local economy.

57. Aldeburgh cod smacks laid up at Slaughden Quay in about 1908. These smacks were laid up during the summer and went longlining during the winter. The prime fish were kept alive in a wet fish well and then landed at Harwich. When the smackmen wanted to get home they often walked, taking the ferries at Felixstowe, Bawdsey, Butley and Slaughden.

58. Very high tide at Slaughden in about 1910. The cod smack laid up in the dock in the centre was Charlie Ward's *Ocean Wave*. Between her and Slaughden Quay, over to the left is the Ground Nut Mill, the shipyard and warehouse and then cod smacks laid up.

59. The Aldeburgh cod smacks were mostly gaff yawl rigged with leg of mutton mizzens. The last of these, the *Gipsy*, sailed on her final voyage in 1913.

60. Belgian children, who stayed at Aldeburgh during most of World War I, being given a trip over the Slaughden Ferry. There was a bell on the Sudbourne shore to summons the ferry. This ferry seems to have stopped in the 1920s, but boatmen regularly put people across until about 1948.

LOADING SUGAR BEET FOR EXPORT ALDEBURGH Nov 26TH 10

61. Loading sugar beet on to a sailing barge at Slaughden in 1910. These sugar beet, which are very small, were being taken to Holland. This was the beginning of sugar beet growing. Because this crop has always had a high labour requirement, it has given a great deal of employment to Suffolk villages during the twentieth century.

62. The peaceful village of Slaughden in 1910.

63. Slaughden from the sea in about 1910. A few posts on the beach are the only defences against the tremendous force of the sea. At the far end is the shipyard, then Ramsbottom's coal store, three cottages built in 1873, Almond's sail loft and fishing gear shop and the 'Three Mariners'. The pub finally closed about 1920 and all these houses went into the sea. In the 1930s some fishermen were trawling over the places where they had once lived. One of the springs which supplied these houses was still on the beach in front of the Martello Tower in 1993.

64. Slaughden in 1910 with the 'Three Mariner's' on the right.

65. A big tide with sea washing over Slaughden and the shingle ridge between sea and river. The 'Three Mariners' is on the left and Anderson's boat building shed in the centre.

66. In 1938 a huge tide swept over the beach at Slaughden. This house, the Hazzard, was on the road between Fort Green and the river wall.

67. The sea washing right over into Fort Green at Aldeburgh in the 1953 Floods. The sea broke through at Slaughden into the Alde, but continual work on the sea defences has held it at bay since.

68. The spritsail barge *Alde* built at Hunt's yard Slaughden in 1882 was the last large craft built on the Alde. The *Alde* was built for Thomas Adamson Riggs who had grocery shops and leased the Aldeburgh Brickworks. Riggs had the barges *Alde* and *Exchange* which took bricks away and returned with rag stone from Kent to repair the river walls on the upper Alde. T.A. Riggs handed the barge over to his son Walter Riggs in 1908. Every summer the barge's hold was swept clear and Walter Riggs and his family went on yachting cruises. These cruises ended after 1913 when Mrs Riggs was drowned from the barge at Slaughden. Three years later the barges were sold.

39

69 (above). Peter Wilson with his 23ft White Wing *Nona*, built 1899, He planned to restore her at the Aldeburgh Boatyard. Serious yacht racing on the Alde-Ore started with the Orford White Wings class. These were originally kept on trots at Shingle Street, but after the Aldeburgh Yacht Club's first season in 1898 the centre of racing moved up to Slaughden. In 1937 the Gare Lochs started to race as a class and replaced the White Wings. The last White Wing raced in 1955, after which the Gare Lochs were replaced by the Loch Longs and Dragons. The only White Wings left in 1994 were the *Quinque*, *Alf-A-Mo* and *Nona*.

70 (left). John Wilson sailing the 15ft Alde class *Rainbow* past Slaughden, 1937. The Aldeburgh Yacht Club introduced the 12ft Red wings class, built at Slaughden by Allen Bros, early this century, and they raced until 1953. The Club replaced these in 1947 with the wooden Lapwing One Design and by 1994 about seventy had been built.

71a. Cliff Hoppitt's view of Slaughden, 1984.

71. Peter Wilson in the original wooden Dragon *Ganymeade* racing past Aldeburgh YC clubhouse in 1974. The Dragons were first raced as a class at the Aldeburgh YC in 1949 and the 21ft Loch Longs started in 1958.

72. The Loch Long class *Astra* and the Dragon *Basilisk* racing in an Aldeburgh YC handicap keel boat race in 1992. Slaughden is a popular centre for yacht and dinghy racing because the bends in the river always provide a varied course with some competitive sailing against the wind.

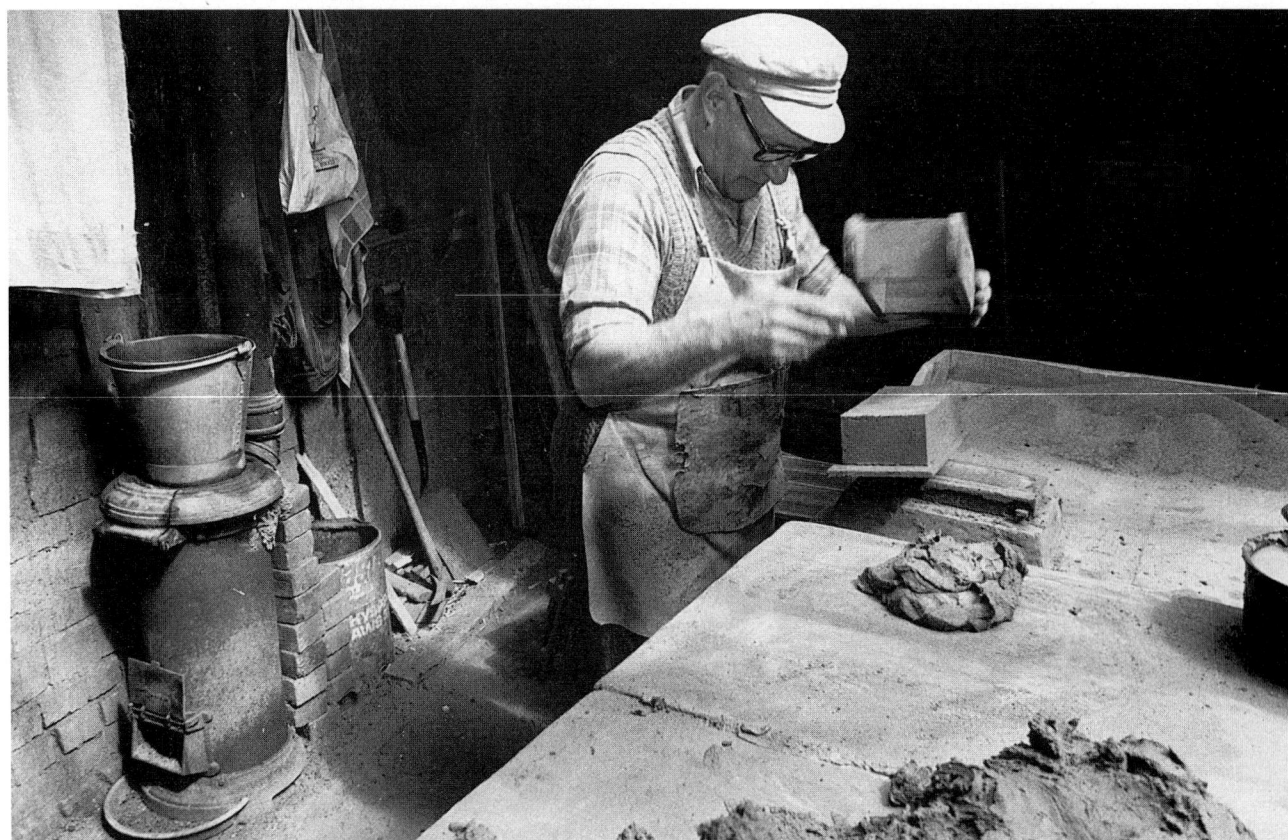

73. Arnold Drew making Suffolk red faced bricks at Aldeburgh Brickworks 1984. He had been working at the Brickworks since leaving the army in 1947.

In the early 1920s Aldeburgh Brickworks, like most of the small local brick fields, was closed, but local builder William Reade reopened it in 1926. When the Aldeburgh Brickworks had coal fired kilns thirty-five men worked here, but when oil fired kilns were installed in 1964 the number dropped to about ten men. The Brickworks had its own clay until 1987, but after this, clay was dug from the old Chillesford brick field pit.

42

## Chapter Five

# PAST IKEN TO SNAPE BRIDGE

74. July 1949. A member of Scolding's gang is placing cement in the toe of the river wall at Iken.

75. A gang putting rag stone above the cement blocks on the river wall at Iken Battle School Area in 1949. During World War II Britain's reliance on imported food created real hardship. There was still food rationing in 1949 so the Government was very keen to meet the cost of repairing river walls to spur on home food production.

76 (below). The tidal surge which created the 1953 Floods swept over all the sea defences on the east coast. Here a USAF plane dips over the Alde. Yarn Hill is down to the right. As it is low tide the salt water can be seen still trapped on the grazing marshes because they are lower than the saltings and ouse which has built up in front of them.

44

77. Sheep, mostly Suffolks, grazing on the saltings below Iken Cliff in 1901.

78. Cliff Hoppitt's photograph showing the Alde from Iken Church to Snape Maltings in 1984. Iken Church is on the site of the Icanhoe monastery built by St Botolph in 654. St Botolph was keen to start his monastery on a remote piece of land so that he did not encroach on other people's property. The present church is built on the site of the Middle Saxon wooden church and the huts of the Saxon monastery were probably just to the south of the church. It is probable that the Icanhoe monastery was destroyed during the winter of 869–70 when a Viking fleet moved up the coast raiding the churches and monasteries and destroying written records.

Late Saxon windows and the shaft part of a commemorative cross dated about 900 have been discovered in the present Norman church. In 1968 the thatched roof of St Botolph's Church was destroyed by fire and services were held in the open for over a decade before it was rethatched.

45

79. Iken Cliff about 1910. Between 1766–1873 George Mingay and then George Rope ran a corn and coal business at Iken Cliff Wharf.

80. Jumbo Ward's Cottage at Iken Cliff in 1965. These red brick cottages are typical of those built in the Suffolk Sandlings during the eighteenth century. When Iken Cliff was a small port the second building was the 'Anchor' Inn until 1886. The original lane to Iken Cliff went past the cottages, but was fenced off by the Suffolk County Council in 1971 to prevent speed boats, used for waterskiing, being brought down here. A popular local move.

81. Mrs Ward right, watching the motor barge *Wyvenhoe* being piloted up river by her husband, 'Jumbo' to the Snape Maltings quay in 1965.

82. Motor barge *Wyvenhoe* passing Iken Cliff bound to Snape with a freight of barley, 1965.

83.'Jumbo' Ward, left, piloting the sailing barge *Lord Roberts*, skippered by Jim Lawrence, up the Long Reach off the Blackheath Mansion on her way to Snape in 1966. The *Lord Roberts*, a barge then converted for carrying holiday parties, was the first sailing barge to go up to Snape since 1939. Snape was one of the most difficult places for a sailing barge to reach. There were cases of sailing barges spending a week getting from Iken Church up to Snape. They just kedged themselves forward a little way on the top of each tide. By the 1920s Vic Brinkley of Orford used his motor boat to help tow barges up to Snape. Some barges were lucky and sailed all the way. The *Beatrice Maud* once sailed light from Yarmouth to Snape in nine hours (one tide) with a northerly wind; while the *Phoenician* sailed, loaded, from the Royal Docks, London to Snape in twenty-four hours(two tides).

84. Snape Bridge in 1904. In 1492 the Bishop of Norwich licensed a hermit to collect alms here to keep the bridge repaired. Later Aldeburgh paid for its maintenance. The humpback bridge built in 1802 was replaced by the present bridge in 1963.

85. Another of Cliff Hoppitt's aerial photographs shows the upper Alde in 1984. This shows the tidal barrier which prevents the tide from going up to Langham Bridge. The track that leads from the front of the Maltings to the corner of the picture was the old railway track which joined up with the main line.

85a. Geoff Cordy's view of Snape Maltings concert hall.

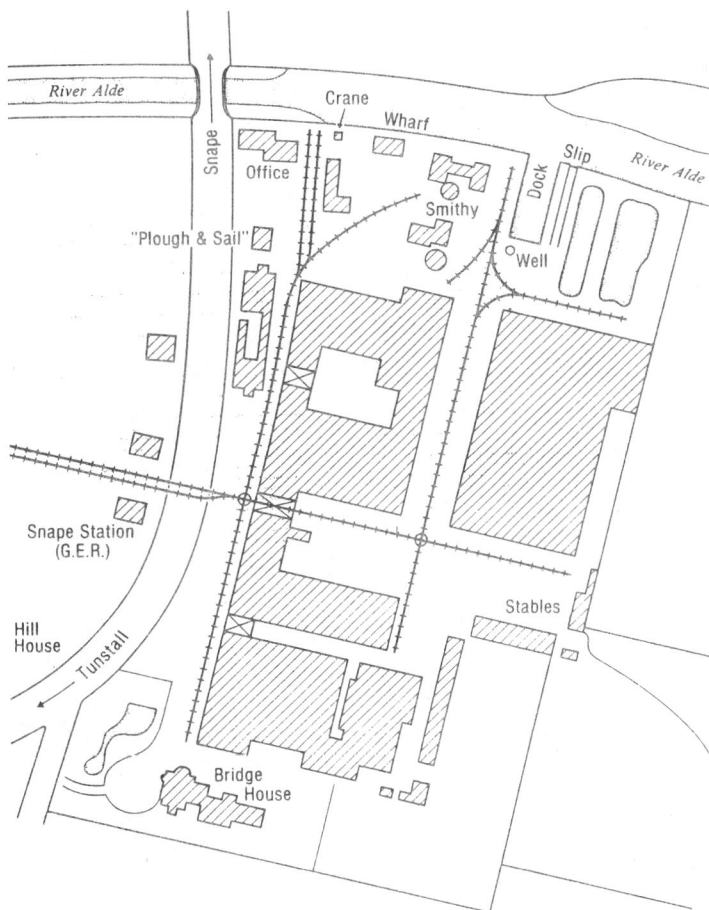

86. Snape Maltings in 1896. In 1840 Newson Garrett bought the corn and coal business at Snape Bridge and also began to build up a fleet of small sailing ships in the coasting trade.

Newson Garrett had part ownership of a brewery in London and supplied it with malt. Snape was well placed to develop the maltings business because the Suffolk Sandlings grew barley which made very good malt and the river allowed transport. In 1859 Garrett had a complex of new maltings built next to the road. For the first building he drew a line with a stick which resulted in a slight curve because he did not walk straight. Snape Maltings was continually expanded and the final malt house (now the Aldeburgh Festival Concert Hall) was built in 1896. The floor method of malting used at Snape went out of use because it was too labour intensive. When the Maltings closed in 1965 forty-two men lost their jobs and the village of Snape was deeply shocked.

87. In 1949 a big tide broke through the river walls above Snape Bridge.

50

88. Between 1865–1960 there was a goods only branch line down to Snape Maltings.

89. The motor vessel *Gillation* arriving at Snape Quay in 1967 with maize from Rotterdam. After George Gooderham bought Snape Maltings in 1965 he started to develop it as a warehouse and revived shipping up the river with the idea of it becoming one of the new ports like Felixstowe.

90. The 103ft, 8ft draft *Gillation* which carried 250 tons and Horlock's *Reminder* at Snape Quay in 1967. Because there was a great protest from Aldeburgh about the increase in road traffic all the material for the Cobra Mist listening station on Lantern Marshes came in from the sea or were shipped down in barges from Snape Quay. This was Snape's brief high point as a revived port.

91. The barge *Redoubtable* arriving at Snape from Woolwich in 1972. George Gooderham bought the *Redoubtable*, converted her back to a sailing barge and kept her at Snape until 1979. The *Redoubtable's* barge's boat is now in the Wine Bar at Snape Maltings.

92. George Gooderham, owner of Snape Maltings, second from the left, surveys the remains of the Concert Hall the morning after the disasterous fire. This happened after the first performance of the third Aldeburgh Festival at Snape. The success of the Festival at Snape lead to the Maltings being developed for tourism.

93. Rebuilding the Aldeburgh Festival Concert Hall at Snape Maltings in 1969. It was totally rebuilt in time for the Festival the following year.

94. The Danish fishing ketch *Zela* being towed up to her new home port of Snape in 1989. Russell Upson is using his 26ft work boat *Spring Tide* which he built in 1983.

95. William Filmer-Sankey, director of the Snape Historical Trust, studying a ring ditch burial at the Anglo-Saxon burial site. Between 1985–91 the Trust excavated this site, half a mile east of Snape church. One of the finds was a burial in a ten foot dugout canoe. In 1862 the local landowner Septimus Davidson had also excavated these burial mounds. He discovered that these mounds had already been robbed, but he did find an Anglo-Saxon ship in which a warrior had been buried.

## ORFORD AND ALDEBURGH RIVER

1. Bella Pond, old channel named after a sailing ship which lies under the shingle near the river wall.

2. North Weir Point. The shingle point at the north of Orford Haven probably got its name from medieval fish weirs (traps) when this point was near Orford. Before 1930 Shingle Street men used to load shingle into barges here. They had special wheelbarrows for going up a plank into the barge.

3. During World War II a road was built so that lorries could load shingle when they built the USAF air base runways.

4. Barthorpe's Creek, medieval Hollesley Haven. The Barthorpe family sold the Hollesley Bay Estate in 1886 to become a Colonial College for settlers going out to new lands in the British Empire. The estate was bought by the London County Council in 1906 and in 1938 became a Borstal and Prison establishment.

5. During World War II a squadron of RAF Air Sea Rescue launches were stationed here. The remains of their old quay is marked by bullets from German air craft. To prevent enemy sea planes landing, this open reach of the Ore was mined during the war.

6. College Dock. Barges used to bring in manure for fields, but the dock was swept away about 1924 by a heavy swell rolling in from the sea. The College Boathouse was destroyed during World War II. After this the Colony landing was used by angling boats belonging to HM Borstal personnel.

7. The Hollesley saltings are owned by the Suffolk Wildlife Trust. The number of open boats kept below Boyton Hall increased rapidly in the 1980s. Boat shed, then moorings appeared.

8. Small gauge railway on the river wall top used during World War II to tow targets out when Boyton Marshes were a tank training area. The Boyton Marshes were bought by the RSPB in 1991.

9. Boyton Dock was built about 1780. Probably because the silting was preventing ships from going up the Butley River. Boyton Dock was used by Minter for barges to ship hay and straw north for pit ponies and return with coal. Wrinch's barges shipped straw out to London until about 1920.

10. When Butley Priory was built, stone was brought to a quay below the Butley Abbey house. The Priory Quay continued in use until the Stonebridge Marshes were walled off in the late 1500s.

11. Barges brought maize up to Hewitt's Butley Mill from about 1900 until 1914. These moored up to a post on the saltings on the bend below the mill and part of the saltings were dug away so that the barges could turn.

12. Butley Mill. The first mill was built in 1530. The mill stopped being driven by water in about 1948 because the river had silted up and John Hewitt could no longer get a good fall of water to drive the wheel.

13. Chillesford Decoy was here in 1790 and in 1907 this was still being used to trap duck for sale. Stopped soon afterwards. Most of the original trees were blown down in the 1987 hurrican.

14. Gedgrave Cliff. In the nineteenth century barges brought bricks and manure here and shipped wheat out.

15. About 1930 a gravel company started to dig shingle from the Orford beach shore and created a large hole. This extraction was banned so they started digging in the area where the Living Huts are on Havergate. The company placed a generator in the Havergate cottage which shook it so badly the place fell down.

16. The Crouch, meaning cross, was probably a beacon here in the medieval period marking the Ore entrance. In the nineteenth century the Stony Ditch mouth was Crouch Harbour.Also in the nineteenth century the Orford Beach Company had their boathouse over on the beach.

17. When Orford Ness was the Atomic Weapons Research Establishment the pagodas were built and used until 1971 to test detonators. The idea was that if the explosion got out of control the 500 ton rooves would fall in and suppress it.

18. During World War II a Bailey Bridge crossed the river from Orford Quay so that stores could be taken to the anti-aircraft guns on Orford Ness. During a hard winter ice came down to Raydon Point and to prevent it destroying the bridge soldiers tried to blow up the ice, but the dynamite drifted down and blew up the bridge.

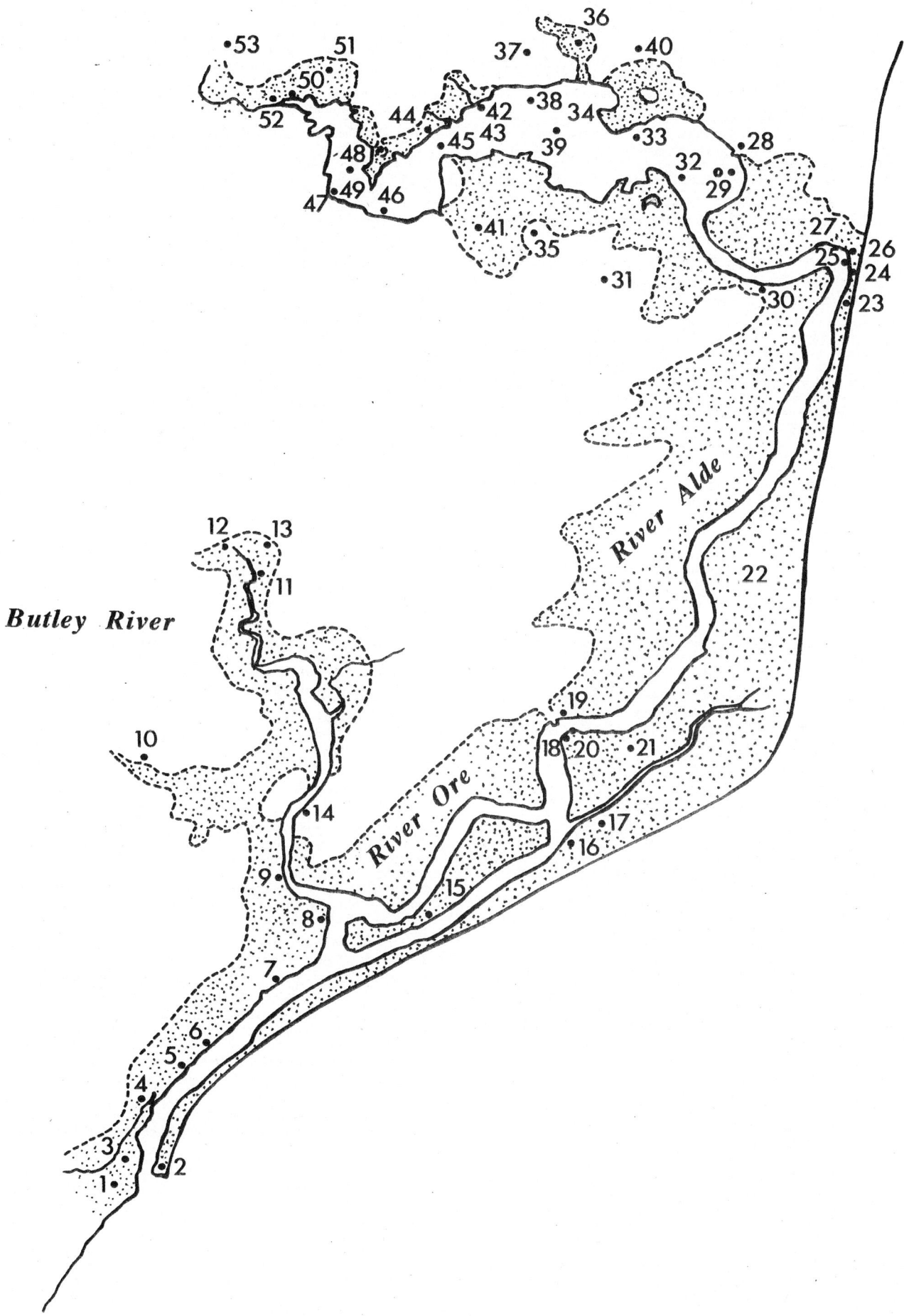

Butley River

River Alde

River Ore

19. The Pavilion is on the site of the Sudbourne Hall Estate boathouse, c1904.

20. Ferry from Orford to serve light house keepers and marsh keepers. The Air Force Quay built to serve the experimental air field on King's Marshes during World War I. Hulk of the sailing barge *Tuesday* which had been used in the 1930s attempt to extract shingle from Havergate.

21. Orford Ness was bought by the Government in 1914 and turned into an airfield. There where a few wooden huts and the planes took off on the grass. The first parachute jump was made here. In 1928 the Island became an experimental station where the initial work was done to discover radar. In 1993 the National Trust purchased five miles of Orford Ness.

22. During the Cold War the United States largely paid for the building of a massive Over the Horizon Early Warning System, code name Cobra Mist. About two hundred masts in the shape of a spider's web were erected on Lantern Marshes. Operational in 1970, but quickly jammed by the USSR. Most of the masts were taken down and the Ministry of Defence leased the site to the BBC World Service.

23. Before 1914 there was a Victorian Shepherd's Cottage well south of the Martello Tower, but it went into the sea. There was also a capstan for hauling up beach boats that also went into the sea. By 1988 the sea had nearly eaten its way through into the Alde and the Government funded the massive sea defences. Granite was brought from Norway in dump barges towed at 2 knots an hour and placed on the foreshore. In February 1993 the sea did just come over the beach to flood the top of the island, but the defences held that time.

24. Aldeburgh Yacht Club is on the site of the shipyard. Cod smacks were being built here in 1784. Three generations of the Hunt family built ships here between 1783–1880. The yard was run for a while after this by H.W. Tilberry. There was a slip at the southern end of the Club house which was buried by shingle in 1953.

25. Slaughden Quay was built about 1542 to replace Thorpehithe at the northern end of Aldeburgh. Allen Bros were boat builders on the quay using the Black Shed which was a World War I aeroplane hanger brought by boat from Orford Ness. Allen Bros left for Wherstead in 1924 because the sea kept burying the slipway with shingle. 1989 Bryan Upson's new workshop.

26. Model yacht pond paid for by Elizabeth Garrett Anderson in 1908 was filled with shingle in the great storm of 1938. Later became Slaughden Sailing Club.

27. Aldeburgh Boatyard was started in 1967 and run by John Gill. In 1979 Peter Wilson took over. The yard was mainly busy with repair and laying up work, but since 1979 many wooden and cold moulded yachts have been built or restored here. About thirty fibre glass Dragons have also been moulded and fitted out here.

28. Brick Dock. Until 1934 Eastwoods barges brought in coal and went out with bricks. From about 1883 there was a small railway down to the dock and it was possible to load three barges at the same time. During World War II the dock was mined so that it could be destroyed if there was a German invasion. In 1944 the Royal Engineers blew up the dock rather than dismantle the unsafe explosives. Yachts were brought ashore during the winter on the railway until about 1953.

29. In 1990 Roman pots were found just above Cob Island on a very low tide. They could have been from a wreck or a crate lost over board. Below this point is one of the places where there is a natural ridge of sandstone across the river bed.

30. Cowton Dock. Nineteenth century barge dock cut in the saltings.

31. The Battle School. During World War II the people living in the lonely villages of Sudbourne and Iken were moved out. Then used as an army training ground for the D Day invasion of Europe. The public were not allowed back into this military area until well after the war.

32. In the 1890s Stanny Creek was still deep enough for cod smacks to be layed up during the summer.

33. Collier's Hole. In the nineteenth century colliers, schooners and brigs anchored here. Their coal was off loaded into lighters and then taken up river. The men unloading the collier schooners used to keep their boats in the Barber's Point sluice.

34. In between 1860–1907 there was a series of archaeological digs on Hazlewood marshes which concluded that there had been a small Roman settlement on a piece of slightly higher ground near Barber's Point. Soundings taken by John Pryor in 1993 showed a stone ridge or ford running from Barber's Point towards Yarn Hill.

35. Yarn Hill. Place of great mystery. Roman pottery found here. Local legend claims that a great battle was fought here. A Victorian account of an Anglo-Saxon sword being found at the foot of the hill. Also earth works on the summit.

36. Before it was walled off Ham Creek ran inland to Decoy Wood and it is probable that the Anglo-Saxon ships buried at Snape would have been dragged up from here. All round Ham Creek eel grass or alva was cut on the saltings by Robert Watson of Rushmere Lodge Farm between 1880–1914 for furniture padding.

37. Sailor's Path used by Snape men going to work, herring fishing at Aldeburgh in the winter and others going to Snape Maltings.

38. Pleasure boat jetty with a dredged channel was built about 1900 for the Vernon-Wentworths of Black heath Mansion. Used by the army in World War II.

39. In 1991 the Suffolk Wildlife Trust rented 350 acres of the mud flats on the upper Alde along the Iken shore and across the river around Ham Creek. These upper Alde mudflats are important at a European level as it is the over wintering home of redshank, black-tail godwit, teal and wigeon. The Trust also bought the Hazelwood Marshes and a car park was created near the road.

40. Hazelwood Street was, in 1885, the area around the ruined cottage. Until about 1860 the north bank of the Alde was open heathland. In the Saxon period, without the trees, it might just have been possible to have seen the Snape burial mounds on the horizon from Slaughden.

41. Iken Decoy was built about 1757 and was a great commercial success. Even in the 1880s about 2250 wildfowl were trapped and sold from here each winter. After James Mann bought the Battle School in about 1951 Iken Decoy was used for sport shooting.

42. Mann's Dock or the Cri'k (creek). This part of Snape Warren was owned by the Bishop of Norwich until 1794. The creek appears to have been a very ancient landing place linked by a track to Friston. It was used by sailing barges until around 1910.

43. Roman salt works. Pans where the river water could evaporate and leave salt.

44. Petter's Hard. About 1880 two stone hards were made so that a sailing barge could lie between them and be loaded from horse and tumbril. This was used up until 1918 when rubbish was brought from London and spread about on the marshes.

45. The Hardway. There appears to be a natural ford across the river from New England Farm to the Iken shore where a track continued to join up with the road at Iken Church. The Hardway could have been used by the Roman settlement on the Iken shore to cross to their salt works. The ford was kept as a local secret and used by the Snape poachers when they raided the great shooting estates on the opposite shore. Game was taken across the ford from Iken and hid on Snape Warren. The poachers then went back across the Hardway and walked home past the police who waited on Snape Bridge. The next day the game was collected from its hiding place and sold.

46. The Oaks. Barges loaded sand for London before 1914. In 1991 Richard Johnson of Iken Hall had old vehicle tyres put in the cliff foot to stop erosion.

47. Iken Cliff. Roman pottery has been found on the foreshore. There are records of ships coming from Newcastle to Iken with coal in 1508. In eighteenth century Mingay ran a coal and corn business here. This was taken over by George Rope who in the 1850s had a schooner sailing each week for London. There was a granary on stilts at the Rope's Cliff Wharf. Rope was supplying coal to the Saxmundham area but stopped using Iken in about 1872.

48. Little Burgh hill on the end of Snape Warren could have got its name, from the Anglo-Saxon 'burgh' meaning fort.

49. Lost hard which was used to drive cattle across from Iken to Snape Warren marshes. There was a dock for sailing barges here. A high tide in 1938 broke through the river walls on the Dunningworth marshes and these were never properly repaired. They returned to tidal ooze. In 1906–07 there were a series of high tides which flooded the Snape Warren marshes. Abandoned in 1923.

50. Snape Dock was the wharf on the north side of the river below the bridge. In 1824 there were quays and ware houses on both sides. Under Newson Garrett's ownership the huge Snape Maltings grew up on the south while Snape Dock fell into disrepair. Sugar beet were shipped out to Holland from here in 1910.

51. Carnser. In Suffolk, farm lanes were often called drifts, but around the Alde a very old Saxon word cansey or carnser has remained for a raised causeway.

52. Snape Bridge.

53. Snape Priory was started here in 1156. There was also a water mill here. Protestant England was so determined to break with the domination of the old religious orders that this large Priory was completely pulled down. However a 13th century Priory barn has survived at Abbey Farm.

# Chapter Six

# THE BEACHMEN

96. Aldeburgh and the River Alde in 1984. Fishing boats were working off Aldeburgh beach in the Elizabethan period and by Victorian times there were 200 men here in the autumn herring and sprat fishery. In 1946 the first fishermen's shed went up on the beach and the pattern of fishing gradually changed. Only a tenth of the former quantity of fish was landed, but the fishermen made up for this by retailing straight to the public. In the 1983 winter there were some thirty men working twenty boats off Aldeburgh beach. Ten years later ten skippers were working their boats, mostly drift netting for sole, and some took on mates for the winter to longline for cod.

97. Brian Cotton and Tom Parnell on Aldeburgh beach getting ready for the summer trawling, 1946. Tom Parnell started off in the Slaughden cod smacks and went on to be skipper of a large yacht in the 1930s

98. Aldeburgh beach in 1990. The boat on the left is Colin Smith's 22ft *Rachael Linda* built by Russell Upson at Slaughden in 1980. Russell took over the lease of Slaughden Quay in 1973 and the *Rachael Linda*, which he designed on the back of a shoe box, was the first boat he built there. These attractive boats with powerful engines were designed to fish up to eight miles off the beach and could tow a trawl on either side. Russell's next boat was the 22ft *Vera* for David Ward. The 22ft *Sarah Jayne* built in 1982 for John Palmer to work out of Southwold harbour introduced hydraulic steering so that the wheel could be fitted amidships and allow single handed trawling. The largest wooden Aldeburgh beach boat,the 22ft 9in *Sheree Ann* was built in 1986 for Willy Free.

99. Percy Westrope and Harry Harling coming ashore in the 18ft sailing beach boat *Industry* at Thorpeness in about 1923. In 1975 Harry Harling, then aged ninety-one was still living at Thorpeness, in the cottage he was born in. Percy Westrup worked the 18ft *Three Sisters* off Thorpeness beach until about 1952.

100. Mrs Brown, Dr Warwick and a beggar man moving a boat at Dunwich in 1905. These 'crab' winches were used at all the Suffolk beach landings before World War II. Every boat had a shore gang of helpers, usually retired fishermen, who helped to get the boats ashore and sort out the nets in return for some fish.

101. Summer visitors watching fishermen returning to Southwold beach about 1905. About forty-five of these boats, known as punts at Southwold, worked off the beach here. Southwold beach was divided up into areas named after the family groups of beachmen that used to work boats from there. Sam May's beach was around the bottom of Gun Hill. Moving north was George Palmer's, then Herrington's and near the pier the Smith family were known as the 'north beach men'.

102. The 49ft yawl *Bittern II*, being launched off the north beach at Southwold. Built in 1890, she was owned by the North Kilcock Cliff Company and crewed mostly by the Smith family. The yawls, pronounced 'yols', were noted for their speed under sail and ablility to survive at sea in terrible conditions. By the time *Bittern II* was built the yawls were mainly being used to race in the summer regattas at the coastal resorts.

103. The 44ft Norfolk and Suffolk lifeboat *Alfred Corry* being launched in a gale off the South Beach at Southwold in 1896 aided by a 'haul off warp' and 'setting poles'. The RNLI boats, crewed by beach-men, took over the rescue work of the old beach companies. The North and Suffolk class lifeboats were the only sailing boats operated by the RNLI because the fishermen insisted on having similar craft to their yawls. The *Alfred Corry*, became a houseboat and was bought by John Cragie, great grandson of her orginal coxswain, in 1977 and restored as a yacht.

104. The Southwold punt *Kingfisher* LT50 got caught on a groyne in 1947 while going out in thick fog. She was worked off the Southwold north beach, just south of the pier.

105. Phil Jarvis going trawling off Dunwich in 1952 in the *Kingfisher*. Phil Jarvis had been in the Royal Navy and in whaling ships before returning to Southwold as a fisherman. He was a well known folk singer in the 'Harbour Inn'.

106. In 1987 Nobby Hutton found a 14ft side rudder, on the beach in front of Easton Broad. This was from a medieval ship of between 900–1100 and was the second side rudder found near Southwold. The first one, carbon dated at 820, had been trawled up at sea. In 1990 pieces of wooden ships were found beside Buss Creek. Believed to be two tenth century trading ships, one with finer lines. Also an unfinished side rudder which lead excavator Valerie Fenwick to believe this might have been an early medieval shipyard site. There is a local tradition that one of the Blyth keels, a vessel that had traded to Halesworth, had been abandoned up this creek.

63

# Chapter Seven

# SOUTHWOLD HARBOUR AND THE LONELY RIVER BLYTH

107. Looking across Southwold Harbour at Walberswick the North Sea herring drifters can be seen hauled ashore for repair, c1870. These sailing drifters were known as 'half and halfers' because the crew took one half of the earnings and the owners, mostly local farmers, took the other half.

108. Two Walberswick herring drifters at Walberswick Quay. In 1870 it was recorded that the North Sea herring fishery was the chief form of employment for Walberswick men. There is a local tradition that the drifters, six smacks and one lugger, were owned in the village and in the summer they went down to the West Country for the mackerel fishery.

109. Men towing a Walberswick herring drifter out of the harbour. There appears to be a wherry in the distance berthed at Walberswick Quay.

110. Looking across to the mouth of Dunwich Creek in about 1890.

111. The 'kissing bridge' over Dunwich Creek, Walberswick in about 1905. There was another foot bridge of this type over the Salt Creek on the Southwold side.

112. Southwold Harbour in about 1984. Traces of the old channels turning south and into the Dunwich River can be seen on the Walberswick Flats.

66

112a. Walberswick ferry landing.

113. Walberswick Flats car park flooded by a big tide in 1993. In the late Victorian times this area was filled in and the fisherman had a large copper here where cotton nets were boiled with preservative to try and prevent them rotting.

114. Southwold men beating the bounds in two of the beach company's rowing gigs about 1900.

115. Tom Spence's Southwold herring drifter *Refuge* entering Southwold Harbour about 1892. On the right some of the harbour pilots are waiting in a boat to help the drifter up to her berth. On the left are anchors brought ashore by the beach companies for resale to ships in distress. By 1994 the channel into the harbour was through the area to the left of the photograph.

116. Fasey's Quay when it was built in 1906 cut right through the shingle knuckle which almost blocked the harbour. Shingle was moved inland from here to fill up the area inshore of the quay. The fish market at Southwold was built because Yarmouth and Lowestoft had become overcrowded by the huge North Sea herring fishery.

117. Scottish fisher lassies having a boat trip in Southwold Harbour. These lassies followed the Scottish drifters south and gutted, salted and packed the herring in barrels for export to Europe.

118. Herring being landed at Fasey's Quay from drifters, both sail and steam. In the foreground are some of the Scottish fisher lassies and the group have been joined by some of the Southwold gentry. On the right, in the distance, is the lifeboat *Alfred Corry*, which was laid up, and the paddle tug *Pendennis* which was brought in by Fasey's to tow sailing drifters into the harbour. They also had a bucket dredger to keep the Harbour open.

119. The first boat from the North Sea fishery landed at the new Fasey's Quay, Southwold in 1907. Soon after this about 300 boats started to land here. Walberswick fishermen 'Dinks' Cooper claimed that as a boy he had crossed the Harbour climbing from one drifter to another.

Here about 35 Scottish boats, mostly zulus from the Moray Firth, are lying in the harbour. Southwold was not popular with the North Sea fleet and the drifters did not come after 1912. The Royal Navy sent torpedo boats here to see if Southwold would be suitable for use in a war with Germany. It is probable that Naval influence overcame local opposition to the building of a branch line which was laid to Blackshore Quay and along the river wall to the empty fish market.

120. The ferryman George Todd with a boat load of summer visitors on the Southwold shore, 1881.

121. The Walberswick chain ferry was operated from 1885–1942. A hand crank was used originally and then this steam ferry. The ferry had to be abandoned because after the 1937 rebuild of Southwold Harbour,the bell shaped mouth funnelled waves up the Harbour which made it too rough for the ferry to operate.

122. Walberswick ferry about 1961 with the postman crossing. During World War II, Frank Palmer restarted the old rowing ferry and this was continued by Bob Cross until his nephew David Church of Reydon took over.

123. 'Sheemo' Palmer's punt (beach boat) sailing down Southwold Harbour in about 1902. Billy English, who lived in the red brick cottage beside the Walberswick 'Bell', remembered counting eighty-seven punts trawling off Southwold in 1927. The fishing grounds within reach of the sailing punts could not support this number of boats and the fleet declined steadily after this.

124. The Blackshore, Southwold just after the 1953 Floods with water pouring back into the Harbour through the breaks in the wall on the Walberswick shore. The former sailing barge *Martin Luther* is opposite one break and the Victorian schooner yacht *Wild Flower* is on the extreme right

125 (above). Devastation on the Ferry Road, Southwold after the 1953 Floods.

126. 'Wiggie' Goldsmith after trawling off Dunwich in his *Johan* LT 103 in 1958 'in the days when there were still plenty of fish on those grounds.'

127. John Winter and his father 'Dusso' Winter with their punt *Dunwich Rose* LT 401 at Southwold in about 1957. The *Dunwich Rose* was a ship's boat that had been washed ashore in about 1920. She was used to take mud up the Blyth for repairing the river walls before being converted for fishing.

128. Joe Palmer mending his beam trawl on the *Arthur & Phyllis* at Southwold in 1970. Joe had had this punt built in 1919 with his gratuity from serving in World War I. In 1994 the only former sailing punts fishing from Southwold were the *Arthur & Phyllis* and the 19ft *Valerie*, both of which had been rebuilt.

129. In the 1930s engines were fitted in the Southwold and Walberswick boats and this made it possible for the fishermen to operate out of the Harbour. The fishermen moved their sheds from the beaches round to Fasey's Quay. In 1946 the Council opened a caravan site on the former Fish Market and net drying area so the sheds were moved again, this time to beside the Harbour.

130. Paul Horsnell's *Joleen* entering Southwold Harbour in 1993. This Suffolk 35 class 120hp nine knot boat was the only Southwold boat to be restricted by a fish quota because of her size. She was used for trawling and longlining up to about ten miles off shore. In 1994 there were thirty six deep hulled and open long shore boats, some of which were worked part time, and four Fast Boats fishing from Southwold.

131. Fast Boats at Southwold, the *Charlotte* LT966 skippered by Roger Doy and owned by C.C. Richardson and the *Prospector II* skippered by Graham English and owned by Roger Desbrough. In 1991 the 26ft 300hp *Charlotte* was the first of the twenty-six knot Fast Boats to fish out of Southwold. Although these boats only went longlining or netting, their speed made them very successful because they could go out beyond the gravel dredger zone to work up to fifty miles off shore.

132. The Blackshore Mill in 1979. This windmill was built in about 1890 to pump the water from the marsh ditches into the Blyth.

133. The Westwood Mill in 1951. This mill was built in 1897 to pump water from Westwood Marshes into the Old Dunwich River. It was working until 1939 and then these marshes were flooded to prevent invading German gilders from landing. The Westwood Marshes became the largest reed bed in Britain. During World War II British army gunnery practice damaged the mill and in 1952 a public appeal raised money and repaired it. It was however set on fire by boys in 1960.

134. RNLI helmsman Derek Kennard on the new inshore lifeboat *D191* at Blythburgh in 1973. In the bow is Katie Gardener who had raised the money to buy this boat.

135. High tide going across the A12 road at Blythburgh in February 1993. This tide flooded the Reydon and Tinker's Marshes for the first time since 1953.

135a. Black headed gulls nesting on the island of saltings on Angel Marshes, Blythburgh 1994. About 600 pairs of black headed gull nest on the Blyth saltings as well as about 15 pairs of redshank and sometimes avocets. By 1989 English Nature had acquired most of the shooting rights on the tidal Blyth. The reduced disturbance greatly increased the number of wading birds that over winter on this small estuary.

136. Blythburgh church, the cathedral in the marshes, is where Anna, the gentle Christian King of East Anglia, was buried. He was defeated by Penda, pagan King of Mercia (The Midlands) at Bulcamp in 654. An Anglo-Saxon minster was built over Anna's grave and the medieval church promoted him as a martyr so that Blythburgh became a place of pilgrimage.

137. The Harbour below Blythburgh Church looking up the Blyth valley towards Halesworth. From the medieval Blythburgh quay the town's merchants sent ships all over northern Europe and to the Icelandic cod fishery.

138. The water mill at Wenhaston in 1925 by Donald Maxwell. The water mill worked until 1930. During the medieval period monks began to straighten the upper Blyth to improve grazing in the valley. They also built a weir at Blyford to prevent the tidal water going any higher. During the construction of the Blyth Navigation, opened in 1761, the river was further straightened and four locks built. At Halesworth the New River section was dug so that keels and wherries could reach the town. The water mill at Mells was pulled down and a new channel dug round Wenhaston Mill. The Wenhaston Mill proved a great problem to the Navigation because of its under shot wheel. The miller wanted the river to be at a low level, while the Navigation needed depth for the wherries. After a long period of dispute the channel to the mill was dammed off so that the water fell about 4ft before going under the Wenhaston Mill wheel. There was a local saying 'go to Halesworth for a new bottom' because the wherries spent so much time scraping the river bed that regular traders were hauled ashore at Halesworth and sheeted with copper plates. In the 1850s about a dozen wherries each loading 40 tons brought goods up from Southwold Harbour. The difficulties of getting ships into Southwold slowed trade down on this Navigation and it was abandoned in 1884.

139. The eighteenth century wallers placed stakes in the bank and then covered them with clay to build the river walls.

# SOUTHWOLD HARBOUR AND THE RIVER BLYTH

1. The bottom of Stocks Lane was the site of the medieval Walberswick Quay. The lane linked it to the original village centre around the church. Elizabethan shipbuilding here and final ship launched was the 28 gun HMS *Baring* in 1654. Great difficulty getting her out of the Dunwich River.

2. Hummerston's Cut. As Easton Ness eroded away Dunwich and its river were also washed away. Around 1464 a new mouth for the remaining Dunwich River and Blyth was cut here.

3. Old harbour mouth. About 1590 Hummerston's Cut was badly eroded and silted up so that another cut was dug to make a new river mouth. During the Elizabethan period there was a ferry across the Dunwich River. The World War II search light unit site is now under the sea.

4. About 1630 the men of Southwold dug out the present site of Southwold Harbour. About 1700 the Dunwich River was dammed to force all the water to go out through the Southwold entrance.By 1745 a sluice was fitted on this river and grazing, with fresh water was established on Corporation, Dingle and Westwood marshes.

5. Granary was the St George boatyard run by Roger De Quincy from about 1946–54.

6. In 1879 a 146ft swing bridge, which turned on a central steel caisson, was built across the river to carry the narrow gauge Southwold-Halesworth railway. The railway closed in 1928, but the bridge remained as a short cut for people on foot. During World War II the bridge was blown up as a precaution against its use by an invading German army.In 1977 the fixed bridge replaced the Bailey floating bridge which had been put across the river in 1947.

7. Angel Marshes were walled off from the tidal Blyth in 1770. They appear to have been abandoned to the tide during World War II.

8. Until the 1870s the 120 ton Southwold schooner *Woodland Lass* brought coal from Hartlepool up to Blythburgh and Baltic timber for Bicker's of Wangford. Sailing barges brought stone for road making until the 1890s. The last sailing barge up here, in 1931, was one converted to a yacht.

9. House boat brought here by Mr Colman from Ipswich about 1948. It drifted up on a high tide and was never floated off.

10. The Harbour below the church is the home for a few dinghies, but this is where local tradition places the medieval trading port.

11. The River Blyth Navigation up to Halesworth was opened in 1761. The Navigation had locks at Bulcamp, Blyford, Mells and Halesworth. This closed in 1884, but about 1900 Fred Lambert purchased the wherry *Star* at Oulton Broad and traded her up as far as Wenhaston until 1911.

12. Marshes north of the Blyth bridge were walled off in 1770 but they flooded after the walls broke in 1926.

13. Bulcamp Marshes. First marshes walled off in 1770 and the outer marshes in 1805. Suffolk Punches from the Henham Hall Estate used to graze these marshes. Lord Stradbroke employed six men to look after the river walls, but when this stopped during World War II the river wall broke. Posts were placed on the marshes during the war to prevent German invasion gliders landing. The Bulcamp Farm jetty was built by the BBC for Simon Loftus in return for filming 'Drowning by Numbers'.

14. Wolsey Bridge. There was a medieval quay at Wangford, but the River Wang was dammed at Wolsey Bridge about 1737. Wharf here for the Lime Kilns and wherries brought coal up here until about 1910. In the 1953 Flood water went across the old A12 road at Wangford. About 1970 the creek mouth was dug again to create a straight channel. The old creek mouth just down river is full of oyster shells.

15. In 1990 fresh water fish in the River Wang were killed by pollution from a factory at Holton. Four years later the Wang had been cleaned up and the National Rivers Authority restocked it with fish.

16. Reydon Quay was built here in 1737 so that ships could avoid paying Southwold Harbour dues. Goods brought down from Halesworth by wherry were also transhipped. Sailing barges worked to Reydon Quay until about 1925 to load hard wood trees. The alder wood quay was pulled down about 1978.

17. Quay Inn was used by workers at Reydon Quay but closed about 1886.

18. Buss Creek, originally Woods End Creek, runs up behind Southwold to a fresh water marsh. The medieval Southwold quay was on this creek. In the 1750s there was a quay here used by the British Free Fishery to collect drinking water. The word Buss Creek comes from buss, a type of fishing craft used in the North Sea by the British Fishery. Several busses are reputed to have been left to rot at the creek mouth. The creek steadily silted up and barge traffic stopped about 1880. About 1960 the Creek was dammed up but it remained part of Southwold Harbour.

19. The Blackshore Quay started about 1630 when the present Harbour mouth was cut and the Town Marshes walled off. The British Free Fishery came here in 1750. The large barn which blew down in 1947, may have been built by the Fishery. The original quay appears to have been in front of the cottages. This was rebuilt and enlarged about 1810. Sailing barges brought in coal for Halesworth and Southwold and wherries brought bricks round from Somerleyton.

20. The first Southwold Sailing Club house was built in 1947 by Eric Paisley and other members on the site of the herring pickling vats.

21. Town Marshes. Because they were owned by the town they were not improved like most of the marshes on Suffolk coast. They remained good wetland bird habitat.

22. The Yard and slipway was the site of Tom Martin's boatyard in the 1930s.

23. Salt works at the head of Salt Creek 1660–1905. Creek was walled when the railway went through to Fasey's Quay.

24. Until about 1939 William 'Ludin' Ladd ran a boatyard, building longshore fishing boats. This area had been the 1906 Fasey scheme net drying ground. When the caravans were moved here the Council created the Square near the Harbour for net drying, but the fishermen soon gave up cotton nets.

25. Trinity water jetty was upstream of Fasey's Quay. Coal for Moy's yard was delivered here by steam coasters until 1939. This jetty and the bridge over Dunwich Creek were damaged by the coaster *Caylx* in 1970 when she broke loose in a NW gale. Southwold Marine Aggregate had a dredger working off the Harbour and the *Calyx* loaded 240 tons of ballast for Rochford..

26. All that remains of the Fish Market is the central wall in the public toilets. Somehow most of the wooden Fish Market was spirited away in the interwar years to become sheds all over Southwold. The large stones laid along the Harbour edge were part of the 1991 Harbour Improvement scheme to break the force of the waves to prevent them from continuing up the Harbour.

27. In the nineteenth century there was a jetty on the beach, probably for unloading ships which could not get into the Harbour and for loading ballast. To the north of the Harbour mouth is the Hale shoal and the South Hams are to the south.

140 (opposite). The Blyth River in 1783. Above the B in Blyth River is Collins' Island. This was formed after the New Cut was dug to speed up wherry traffic to Halesworth.

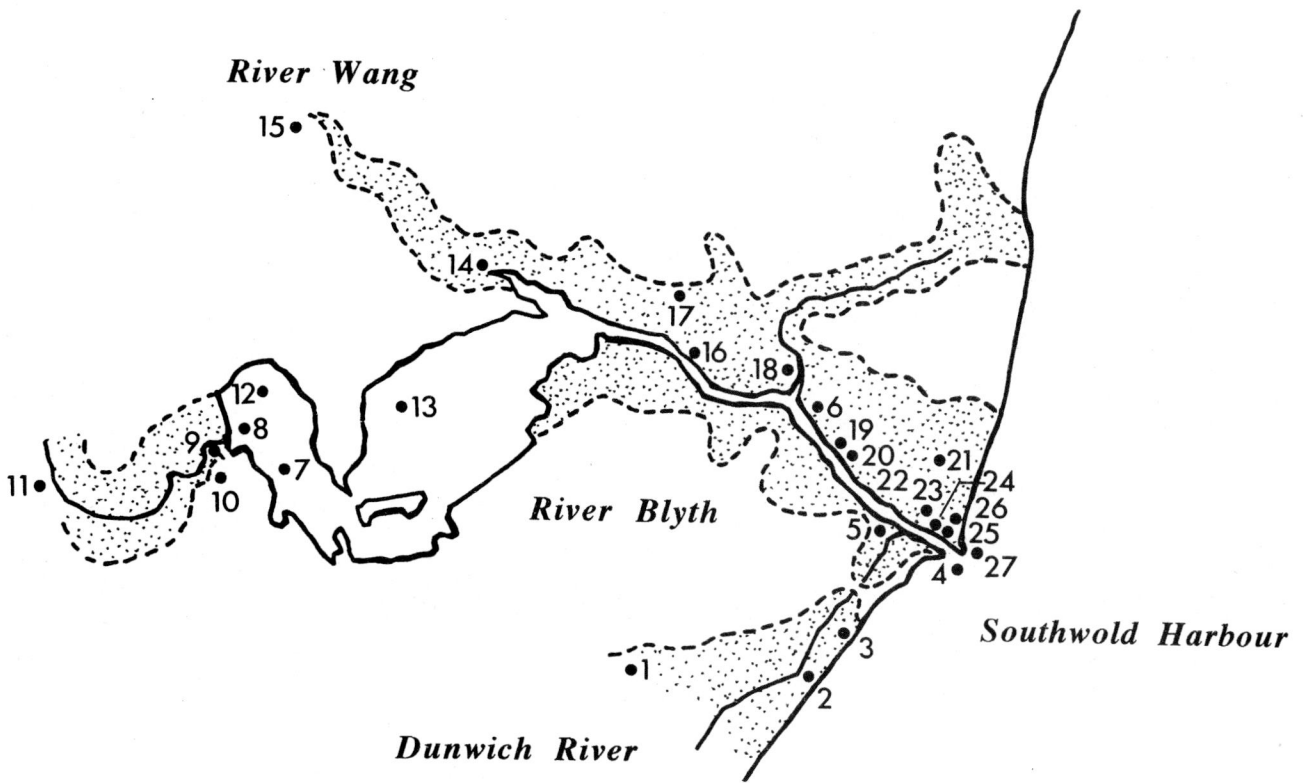

River Wang

15

14

River Wang

17

16

18

12

9   8

13

6

11

7

19

10

20

21

22 23   24

River Blyth

5   26

25

4   27

Southwold Harbour

3

1

2

Dunwich River

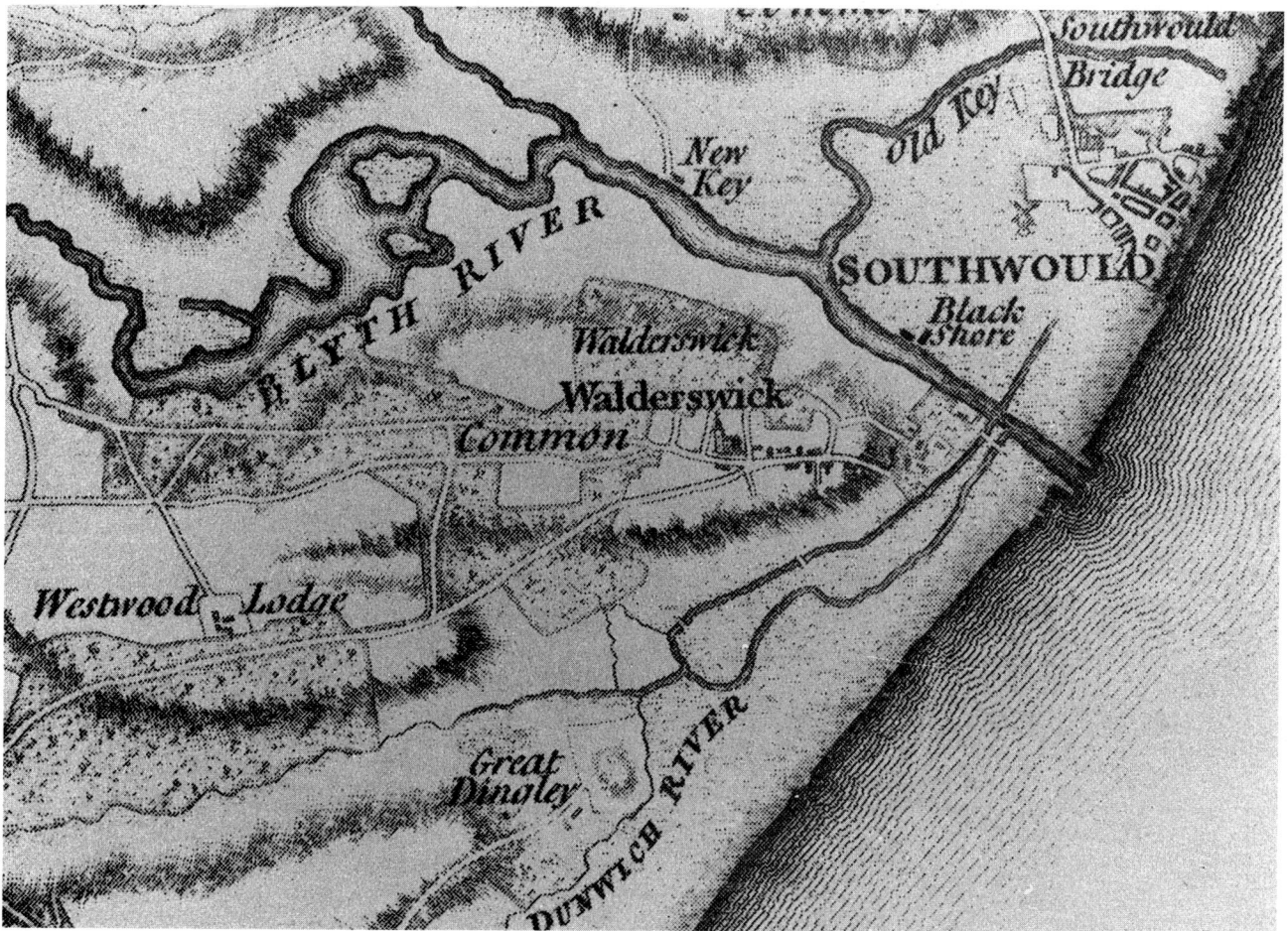

141. This part of Dunwich beach and the sheds on it were washed away by three large storms during the winter of 1911–12. Most of Dunwich was lost during severe storms, but over 700 years an average of a metre a year has been lost.

142. The beach village below the cliff at Southwold about 1905 before the sea ate it away. The Suffolk coast and rivers have an age old battle against the encroaching sea, but winning financial support to maintain effective defences is an even greater problem.